This Colorig Book Belongs To

Copyrights 2019
Mahmoud Osman

AMPHIBIAN

ANIMAL PAT

DEVIL

BROOMSTICK

mistletoe

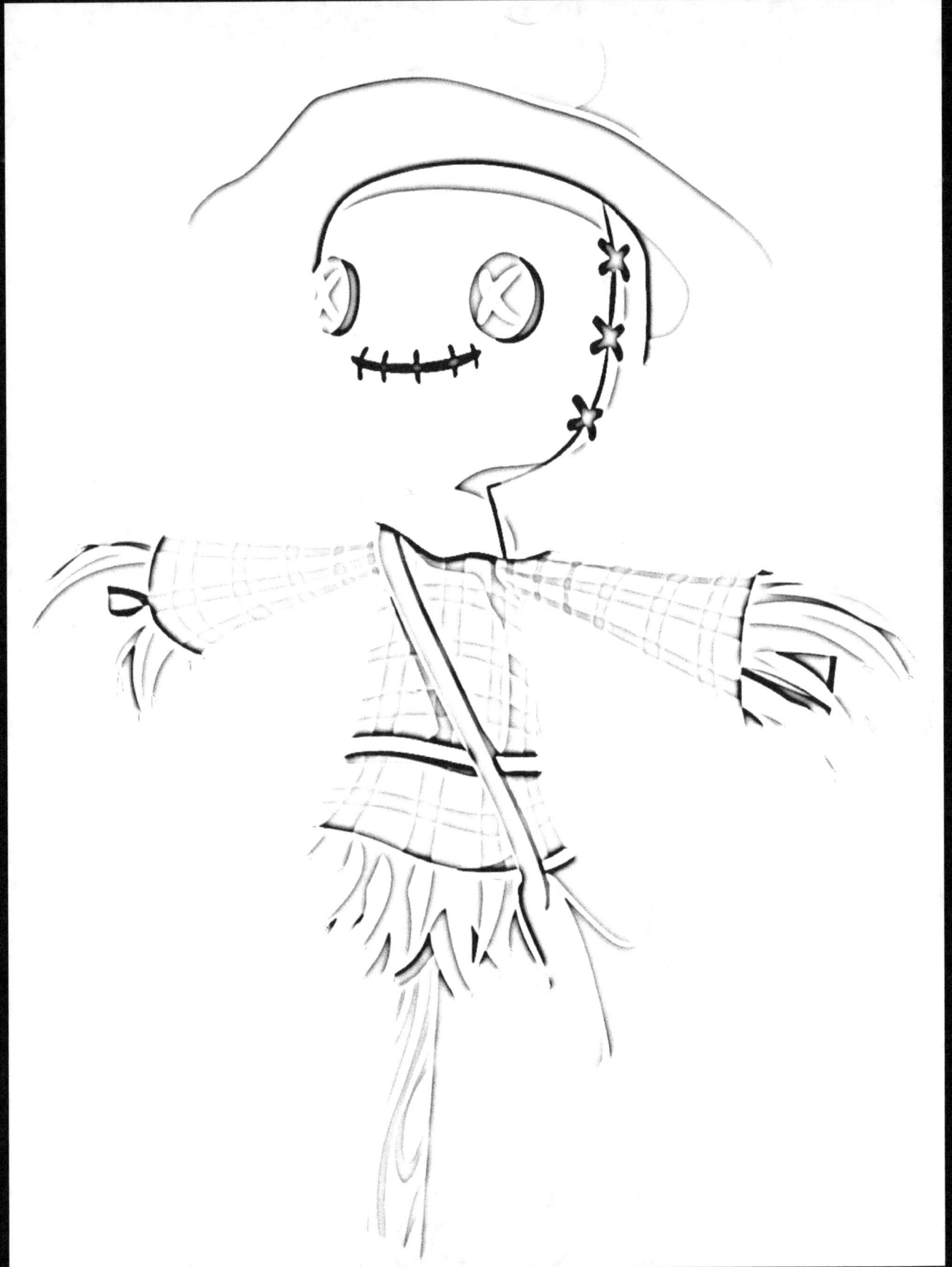

guard

hallwoeen boy

BUMPKIN MAN

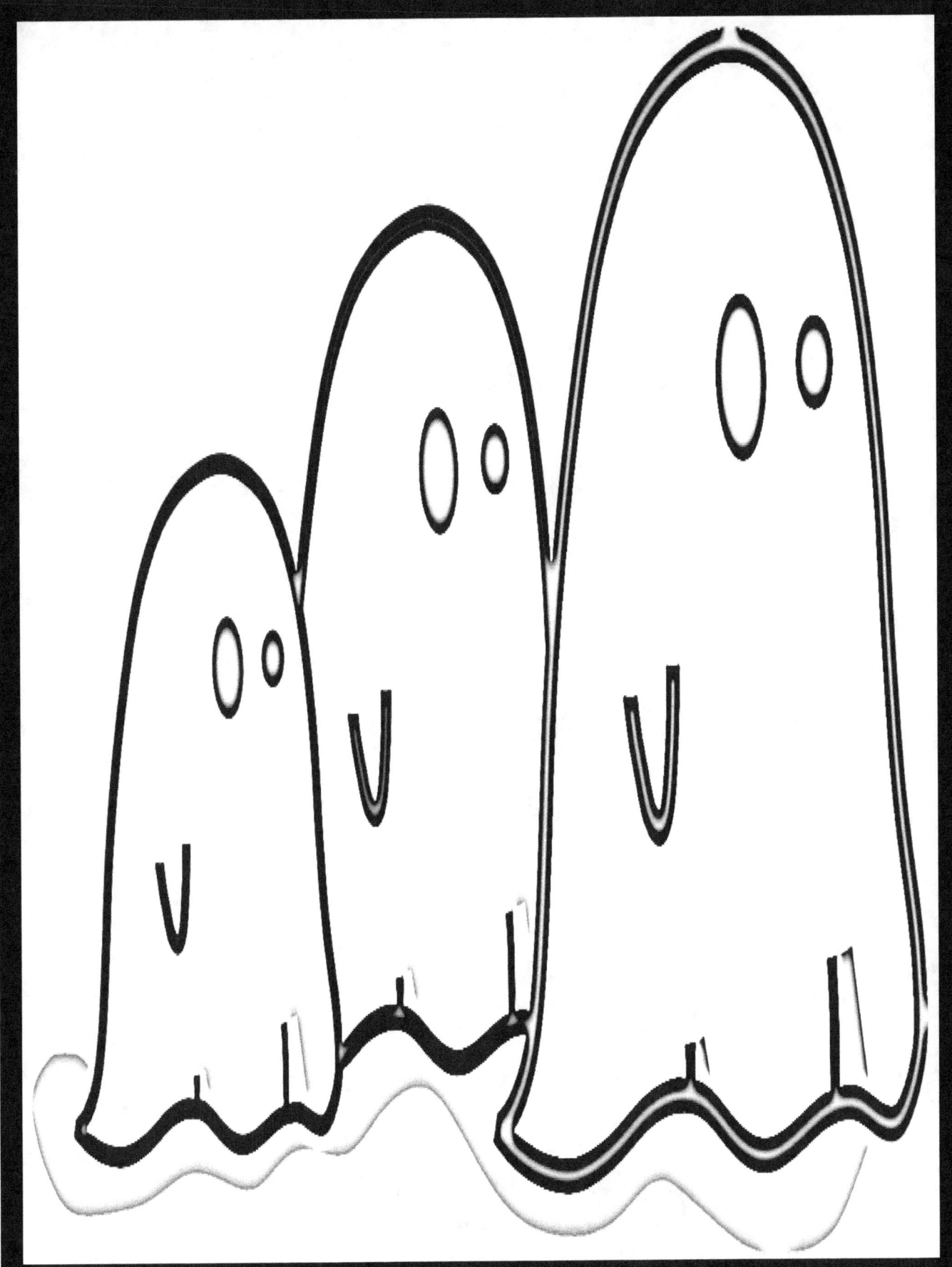

BOO GHOST

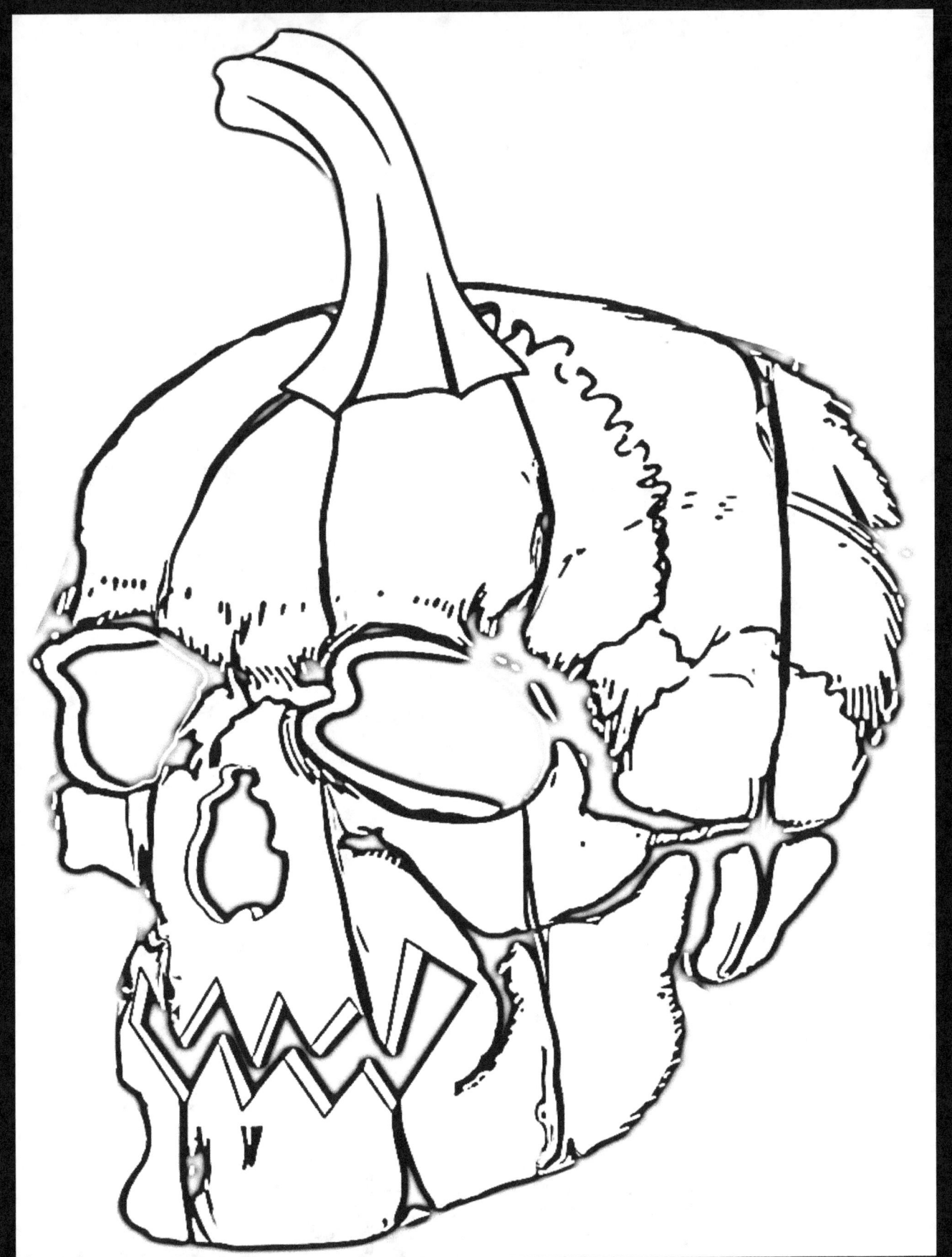

BUMPKIN SKULL

bumpkin

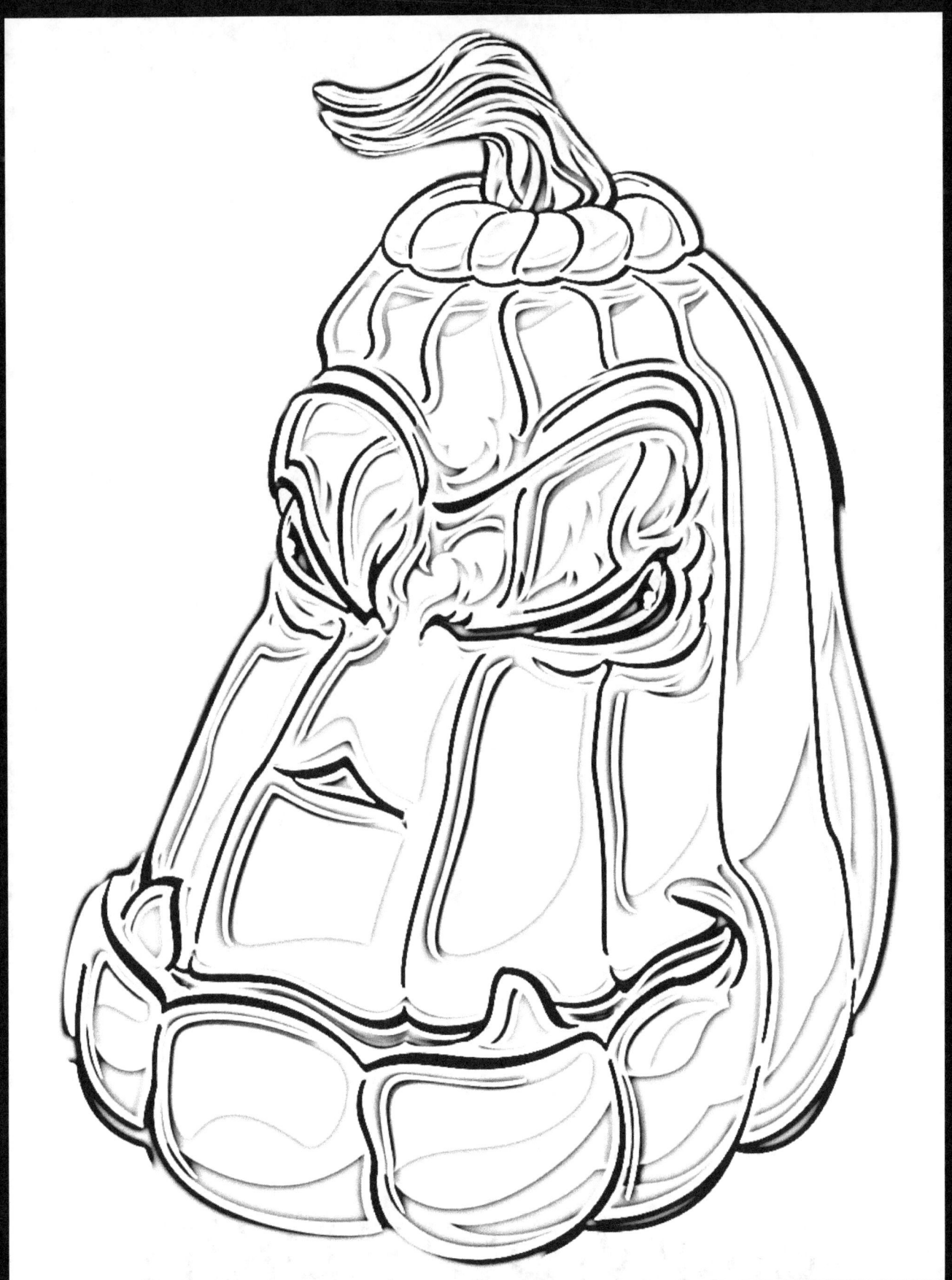

angry bumpkin

WITCH

hallwoeen is cream

www.ingramcontent.com/pod-product-compliance
Lightning Source LLC
Chambersburg PA
CBHW081708220526
45466CB00009B/2919